Seeking and Surrendering

Poetry on Soul, Self,

and a Puzzling Life

Seeking and Surrendering

Poetry on Soul, Self, and a Puzzling Life

Parto Dehdashti, Ph.D.

Published by Wondering By The Lake, LLC

For permission and licensing requests, write to the publisher:

Wondering by the Lake, LLC
153 Sugar Belle Dr, Suite B-111
Winter Garden, FL, 34787
www.wonderingbythelake.com

ISBN: 979-8-9895046-1-9   (paperback)
ISBN: 979-8-9895046-0-2   (e-book)

First Edition 2023.

Cover design by Parto Dehdashti.

The poems contained herein may not be suitable for all readers and are not given as advice. Neither the publisher nor the author shall be liable for any actions or inactions of the readers. The poems are not about any one person, place, practice, or belief but are purely poetic expressions about life. They do not necessarily represent the author's personal beliefs.

Special thanks to my parents for having been pillars of love and strength, and to my family and friends for standing by me throughout the years.

Additional thanks to those who provided feedback on the early drafts of this book: Annette Bonner, Carol Anderson, Jeffrey Jones, Niki Abrishamian, and Nooshfar Katooli. Thank you for your willingness to read the book and for providing your valuable suggestions and unique perspectives.

Contents

Table of Contents

Preface

This private collection of poems is being offered for the first time. The book is a compilation of poetry seeking answers over the years, sharing a puzzled view of life. The inspirations have come from thought provoking books, beautiful sceneries, observations, conversations, dreams, and moving events. The poems reflect how I have absorbed, interpreted, and felt those inspired moments.

The poems share struggles in understanding self and life with their innate conflicts and reconciling the here and now with what is larger than the story of humanity. The moments of darkness and light have sometimes been intertwined, indicating how much we can affect our own state of mind. Similar and contradicting concepts among and even within the poems, indicate perplexity and growth. In search of spirituality, the answers have been evading me, but a few precious moments of clarity may be sensed in the poems. Some poems may feel melancholy, and others insightful, enabling a spiritual connection and hopefully, letting go of what holds us back.

This book is organized in four chapters, each with poems similar in theme. The themes capture the essence of the poems, but there is a general premise of seek and surrender spread throughout the book.

> The *Puzzled By Norms, Rules, and Roles* chapter represents grappling with sociocultural choices, expectations, obligations, and judgments. Strong moments of frustration as well as hope and recognition of how precious is this chance on life are woven in.

The **Seeking** chapter is focused on the confrontations with ego, search for the soul, the quest for spiritual discovery and the entangled reach for the elusive enlightenment.

The **Appreciation and Connection** chapter represents moments when the beauty of the gifts we are given were most strongly felt.

The **Part Of A Whole** chapter represents moments of broader awareness of what is visible or invisible, real or imagined.

Although the chapters provide an organization to the poems, you may read the poems in any order you wish.

Some of these poems may be meaningful to you and resonate with thoughts or experiences you may have had. Other poems may seem out of the ordinary and difficult to grasp. Either way, hopefully, they will convey the importance of finding one's own way to be more in tune with one's self, soul, and the universe.

Thank you for spending these once private moments with me. Perhaps, it was meant to be that I am sharing these poems with you, in this moment in time. May we all find what we seek and relish the ride along the way!

Puzzled By Norms,
Rules, and Roles

Puzzled By Norms, Rules, and Roles

Your Circle

The boundaries that we set
The circle that surrounds each

The rules that guide us
The rules that bind us

The goals trapped within the circle
The hopes lost within the circle

...

Break the circle
Clear the path

Fly over
Dig down inside

...

That circle is unreal
That rule is unbinding

Find your true self
Fight for its release

Seeking And Surrendering

Be true to your soul
It's broader than the circle

...

Break the circle
Clear the path

Fly over
Dig down inside

...

Your guide is within you
Trust the voices

Your heart is true
Trust the dream

You're all there is
There are no limits

All Of That

So many roles to play in life
So many duties to fulfill

Some roles we wear well
Other roles wear us down

Unfit roles seem exhausting
Taking missteps are disheartening

Conflicts devour our lives
So many days seem lost in the roles

...

Every step builds on the other
Every experience helps the next

What I am today is as it should be
What I will be tomorrow is meant to be

Don't waste a lifetime in doubt
Take each moment and build on

Seeking And Surrendering

Breathe deep, play hard
Every minute is a gift of love

Take charge and surrender
Hear your spirit, whispering at night

You are all of that, and then more
Ready to listen, ready to feel, ready to believe

Worth The Time

Day to day
Month to month
Year to year
A lifetime

A nice car
A nice house
A nice family
A nice job

A football game
A baseball game
A tennis match
A running path

A broken bike
A leaky roof
A worn-out knee
A bad review

Washing dishes
Tending the garden
Staying healthy
Giving to charity

Seeking And Surrendering

Collaborations
Friendly neighbors
Family time
Loving someone

Fighting traffic
Fighting a cause
Fighting for your life
Fighting a war

Playing in the back streets
Seeing stars under the dark sky
Flying to space
Discovering planets

...

What's worth my time?
Worth the experience?
Worth the days I live life?

The job or the spirit
The dishes or the causes
The game or the discoveries

Puzzled By Norms, Rules, and Roles

What's visible?
What's beyond?
What's the truth behind it all?

Do I have to know?
Do I have to choose?
Can't I stay in the unknown?
Can't I go with the flow?

I'll take the chance to experience a worthwhile life

Seeking And Surrendering

Gladiators

Gladiators racing in the stadium
Fighting to win
With no mercy to spare
Being at their best, taking charge
Roaring with hunger, rage
Achieving, succeeding, destroying along the way

What spectacle, with what grandeur
Showing off, being at their best
Entertaining the leaders, the masses
Being heroes for the moment
Winning with passion
Winning the riches

In the stadium of life
Are we all spectacles?
Doing our best with the given gifts
But, no matter at what cost?
Are we the hunted or
The masters of our own theater?

Puzzled By Norms, Rules, and Roles

Who is organizing?
Who is keeping score?
Who is watching?

Who is cheering?
What is worth the fight?
What is worth the win?

Seeking And Surrendering

Ordinary

All those plans, all those measures
Where do you put your heart?
Organized, all things checked
Where is the pause?

You know what you did last month
You know what you'll do next month
Yet dragging, anxious, restless, bored
Breathing harder and harder

Fearing the unknown, fearing failure
Predictable, reliable, uninspiring
Pushing forward, seeking comfort
Ordinary is such a predator of the soul

Ready yet for change?
To feel the mystic breeze?
Chancing it all?
Taking the risk?

Puzzled By Norms, Rules, and Roles

You were sold a dream
It is not yours to keep
Throw it away
Open the flood gates

Where would you go?
What would you do?
How would you know?
How would you feel?

Break the barriers, test the waters
Dance barefoot into the cold, into the heat
Free flow far beyond the end in sight
Lunge to the unseen distance

Release all that you are
Surrender to the unknown
You'll be true to your authentic self
You'll be amazed by your loving soul

Seeking And Surrendering

Bending Branches

If I bend, will I fail?

Will I lose myself?

Will I forget?

Will I break?

Will the walls tighten around me?

If I bend, will I learn?

Will I find myself?

Will I remember?

Will I embrace?

Will I see beauty all around?

If I bend will the wind hear my cries?

Will the rules start shattering?

Will the voices stop holding me back?

Will the flowers start blossoming?

Will space still shine with stars?

If I bend will the sun be brighter?

Will my powers grow stronger?

Will my tears turn to pearls?

Will my heart fill with love?

Will my self be whole again?

For What?

My purpose is unknown
My days spent on the ordinary
The pain is overwhelming, piercing, agonizing

One day after next
Busy being busy
A life seemingly uninspired

Days turn into nights
Nights turn into nightmares
No sleep for this restless soul

Working for stature, wealth, possessions?
Looking for clothes, new cars, new friends?
Caring about better health, longer life, worthy cause?

If all an illusion, why play the game?
Why bother with hope?
Why feel all this pain?

Taking one day at a time
Nothing to lose, nothing to gain
Living aimlessly, living in a daze

Seeking And Surrendering

All this effort, what's the prize?
Nothing worth reaching for
Nothing worth fighting for

The fog is encircling me, blinding me
Self-absorbed, my shadow tightens its grip
This sadness is overwhelming, with no answer in sight

All the expectations that cripple me, torture me
Unnecessary fears that consume me
Wasting precious little time ticking away

Yearning to be worthy and heal
I start seeing the extraordinary that surrounds us
The love that's in every particle making us whole

Believing in the benevolence
Believing in the grand design
Faith is all I need to carry me thru the fog

Living, absorbing, surrendering
Hoping, sensing, knowing
Slowly the fog lifting, sun shining, rainbows flying

Puzzled By Norms, Rules, and Roles

Rules In My Head

Rules in my head
Scaring me
Failing me
Hurting me
Slowly drowning me

...

Crossing them off
Erasing them
Black marking them thick

...

Becoming alive
Balanced again
Opening up
Feeling connected
Loving all

Seeking And Surrendering

Obligations

Obligations
Sacrifices
Desires

All too much
Seems impossible?

...

Abundant Love,
Divinity,
Serenity

All encompassing
All possible

Puzzled By Norms, Rules, and Roles

Tired

Tired of these arbitrary divisions
Tired of the pretenses
Tired of the delusional justifications
Tired of fights crafted in the head
Tired of the pointing fingers
Tired of the misunderstandings
Tired of it all in the name of politics, religion, or whatever

...

Wishing wisdom
Wishing empathy
Wishing understanding
Wishing forgiveness
Wishing kindness
Wishing generosity
Wishing love

Seeking And Surrendering

Heal Ourselves

Today, here, and now
There's enough goodness in the world
To conquer the malice we see

So many smiling faces filled with joy
So many hugs padded with affection
So many uplifting stories to fill each lonely night
So many giving hearts showering those in need
So many well wishes from deep inside

Let's join hands
Believe in us
Build together
Heal ourselves, our minds, our souls

Let's revive the tender human heart
Let's protect each and give blessings to all
Let's be the love we want to feel
Let's share the abundant gifts that surround

No matter who, what, where, or when
Our love is more than enough
To restore the souls of those who've lost their ways

Puzzled By Norms, Rules, and Roles

A Person First

When you look at me, Who do you see?
The person or the visible?

Maybe I get too mad
Or don't fight back

Maybe I'm too thin
Or weigh too much

Maybe my color is unlike yours
Or my eyes are unusual

Maybe I don't come from where you were born
Or don't pray in the same way

Maybe I'm too rich and successful
Or think I know the answers to your questions

Maybe I don't have a job
Or my work is not done in a suit

Maybe my words frighten you
Or they inspire you

Seeking And Surrendering

Maybe I'm insecure
Or too confident

Maybe I'm a team player
Or a recluse

Maybe I'm on the far sides
Or prefer the middle path

...

So many differences to help us grow
So many parallels for shared understanding

Let's look beyond the visible
And grasp beyond what we see

What divides us is the splendor of creation
What defines us, are stories to be heard

Do you know why I am who I am?
Can you see inside my soul?

We each are a person first
And that's who I ask us to know

Puzzled By Norms, Rules, and Roles

Freedom

Let Freedom truly be

Let me feel the air without a fearful breath

Let me dance in the streets flying high

Let me raise a flag, any flag, but mostly white

Let me see your land, wherever you are

Let me share my beliefs, crazy or righteous

Let me shake your hand, color blind, color aware

Let me sing in my native tongue, or sing with you

Let me say any thought, without retribution or judgment

Let me get wet in the rain, and burn under the sun

Let me hear you out, whichever side you are

Let me feel pain and joy, to live life

Let me be me, whoever I need to be

Let me catch my breath, slow my heart, watch the clouds go
    by

Let me live, let me love, let me meet my soul

Let me be one with you, anywhere, anytime

Let me be free of you, with you

Seeking And Surrendering

Maybe It's About

Maybe it's not about how much you have
How much you earn
How much you keep

Maybe it's not about you
Who you know
Who knows you

Maybe it's not about your lovers
Your followers
Your friends

Maybe it's not about your parties
Your jobs
Your titles

Maybe it's not about your looks
Your color
Your gender

Maybe it's not about your rules
Your religion
Your habits

Puzzled By Norms, Rules, and Roles

Maybe it's about how much you helped
How much you created
How much you gave

Maybe it's about how much you felt
How much you listened
How much you shared

Maybe it's about how much you loved
How much you cared
How much you cried

Maybe it's about how much you tried
How much you learned
How much you taught

Maybe it's about the experience
The generous blessings abound
The awareness

Maybe it's about your soul
The connectedness
Your Oneness

Seeking And Surrendering

Nonsensical Games

These games we play ...

They hold me on a leash
Compel me to follow
Mindlessly pursuing
One more, one more ....

Winning rewards me
Puts the spotlight on me - but for a moment
Losing shames me
Darkens my days - for all time

Do this
Do that
Less of this
More of that

End these nonsensical games
These unbearable time-wasting routines
These endless loops of duties, rituals, and demands
These made-up rules that spellbind us to obedience

Puzzled By Norms, Rules, and Roles

Cut this noose that's around my neck
Undo this rope wrapped around my hands
Peel this tight tape clasping my lips
Release these imaginary hands that hold me down

Let me be free of obligations
Free of the rules
Free to form
Free to see

Let me become ...
Inspired
Boundless
Fearless

Let me open my arms
Filled with love through eternity
Flowing like a river
Playing in the sand of time

Let me play a new game
With no winners, no losers
Amazed at every turn
Living, learning, whirling, growing

Seeking And Surrendering

Binding with the sun and the moon
With the ocean and the land
With metal and stone
With air and fire

All is good in this game
Loving, joyous, eternal game
I feel free
I feel Love

Narrow Path

This narrow path has no room for error
Has little room to grow

Sometimes seems straight and smooth
Other times rough, yet still so narrow

I want to feel the extremes
Swing with the wind

I want to touch the rose's thorns
Navigate the rapid waters

I want to take the shortcuts
Follow the hidden paths

I want to diverge and converge
Stay calm and burst into feelings

...

But whatever the path
No matter how narrow or wild

Seeking And Surrendering

My destiny is my story
My story is my destiny

I have to feel what I feel
Be who I am

It's a ride I meant to take
No matter how the path is laid

All that I seem to control and controls me
Is still my narrow path to live

I'll enjoy the beauty of the path and
Stay amazed at the Mastermind

Puzzled By Norms, Rules, and Roles

Burdens We Carry

We all have burdens we carry
From discrimination to missed opportunities
From prejudices to aggressions
From hatred to atrocities
All for "justifiable" reasons

So many places, traditions
So many races, faces
All on the planet earth
All from one source

We all have burdens we carry
Holding us back in fear
Piercing into our hearts
Feeling blamed, disrespected, abandoned
Shaming us to submission, to bury our gifted selves

We carry the burdens of our ancestors as ours
Some, hide in the comfort of the known
Hoping not to be found
We are all one, living for love
Living for a connection that has no bound

Seeking And Surrendering

We risk our lives for freedom
For a chance of a better life
We work hard to fit in
To succeed, to be worthy of the chance
Yet, we long to belong

We are born members of the cosmos
We are one in the brilliance of life
We are coded to each other
We are from the history that is behind us
We are from the future that is yet to be lived

Our lives are intertwined
Won't you be a friend?
Helping us grow together
Sharing the paths
Helping us feel welcomed

Believe that we are one
Help us carry our burden
Help us build a life filled with love
Help us unburden the future for all
Let us love

Sleepwalking

How did you use your days?
Your nights?

How much did you use your might?
Your gifts?

Did you push yourself for another book to read?
For another lesson to learn?

How often did you try something new?
To feel the uncertainty?

How much did you try to live?
To treasure each day?

Did you try to create anew?
To add to the abundance?

How much did you listen?
And hear the god within?

How much did you feel?
The pain of the living?

Seeking And Surrendering

Did you try to love?
Or mend broken hearts?

How much did you question the game?
And see beyond the rules?

How much did you join with the One?
To feel your natural greatness?

Did you miss life with a blink of an eye?
Or did you live?

Did you stay awake?
Or did you sleepwalk?

It's not too late

Puzzled By Norms, Rules, and Roles

Looking Back

Thinking about my end,
Looking back at my lifeless body, what would I feel?

Would I remember years of happiness and sadness?
Would I be at peace with what I have done?
Would I be proud of the person I was, if pride has meaning?

Would so many years of work still seem important?
Would I care that I created value?
Would the possessions I left behind bring joy to anyone?

Would I say I respected enough and treated all fairly?
Would I say that I was a good child, spouse, and parent?
Would I say my friendship put a smile on our faces?

Would I say that I learned enough?
Would I say that I did not waste my days?
Would I say that I did my best and it was good enough?

Would I think that I touched anyone's life?
Would I say that I loved enough?
Would I believe I made a difference with my causes?

Seeking And Surrendering

Would I say that I was true to myself?
Would I say that I felt alive and awake?
Would I say that I felt one with God?

Would I feel connected to the cosmos?
Would I become a guiding light?
Would I know the truth?

Seeking

Seeking And Surrendering

The Why

Would it make a difference,
If you knew the why?

Would you feel freer?
Would you scream with joy?
Would you treat all with an open heart?

Would you view the world with a different lens?
Would you live each day more fully?
Would you see the angels all around?

If you knew the why,
Who would you be?

Why not live and love more?
Believe in the unseen,
Even if you don't know the why?

Seeking

Empty Inside

Release me from this pain
Restless, unaware, uncertain

Empty inside
Breathing to no end
No truth
No enlightenment
Selfish and sensitive
Hurt and lost
Ordinary and empty
Wasted minutes, wasted days, wasted life

Empty inside
Burning to sense
Whirling to feel
Reading to know
Living to experience
Seeking bewildered
Yearning for a peaceful mind
Wasted minutes, wasted days, wasted life

Seeking And Surrendering

Empty inside
Wishing for one glimpse
For one moment of clarity
For knowing the truth
For joining with the one
For feeling connected
For seeing beyond
Wasted minutes, wasted days, wasted life

Empty inside
Closing my eyes, once more
Breathing deeply
Calming down
Feeling peace near
The moment is here
Nothing wasted

Rejoicing with love
Tranquil, aware, on path

Un-Frazzle

Un-frazzle me
Unchain me
Grant me clarity
Grant me peace

Break me free
Calm my soul
Help me smile
Help me be love

Untangle me
Unwind me
Help me breathe
Help me fly

Connect with me
Trust in me
Clear my path
Guide me through

Help me see the light
Enlighten me
Let me be the light
Empower me

Seeking And Surrendering

Swirling

Swirling in bewilderment
Turning to rhythm

Searching for the divine
Surrendering, crying

The elusive enlightenment
Internal, within

Infusing, absorbing
Swirling, swirling

Seeking

No Coincidence

It is no coincidence that I am here
That we are where we are

We work hard towards our goals
To keep the control

People pass us by
Days turn into nights

We go on as though life is a habit
That there is always a tomorrow

Sometimes we ponder- is this all there is?
But soon, the mind goes back to mundane little things

My destiny is in my hands
Your destiny is in your hands

We search until we find our truth
Until comfortable with how we see life

The world goes around with or without us
The world goes around as it is its fate

Seeking And Surrendering

Does this sound confusing?
Does this sound contradictory?

I am bewildered, but life will go on
And this is no coincidence

Seeking

Within These Walls

Within these four walls
I scream at myself
Yet, I hear no sound

Within these four walls
I look in the mirror
And I see a desperate set of brown eyes

Within these four walls
Day or night make no difference
The despair is blinding like a dense fog

Within these four walls
I move a hand, I blink an eye
Yet, there is nowhere to go

Within these four walls
I wonder if there is God, I wonder if there is hope
There are no miracles for this tired soul

Seeking And Surrendering

Within these four walls
I can only imagine what the world is like
My fearful being can't dream of a better tomorrow

Within these four walls
The window is dirty, and the door is locked
I see the key, yet why bother try

Seeking

Let Me Be

Ego strongly taking hold
Suffocating me
Fooling me with pretenses
Enticing me with the worldly
Feeling empty, unfulfilled
Can't stop drinking this poison
An addiction unbearable, unstoppable

Grasping for air
Grasping for hope
Turning into quietness
Reaching into my soul
Surrendering
Emptying with hope
Breathing, waiting, breathing

When will I be blessed?
When will I be touched?
Ego is so strong
Unbending, relentless
Grabbing hold of me
Drowning me again

Seeking And Surrendering

Grasping for air
Grasping for hope
Turning into quietness
Reaching into my soul
Surrendering
Emptying with hope
Breathing, waiting, breathing

The cycle continues
... yet, hope is there
Keeping me aware
Helping me cope
Keeping me afloat
Believing in the unknown
Believing in being me, my soul

Seeking

Sync

Out of sync
Out of touch
Unbalanced, insignificant, and lost

Walking in the fog,
With mirage of a path

Walking on the edge
Taking missteps at every turn

My heart is pounding
My thoughts are racing

Nowhere to go
But hide in the trenches

...

I hear whispering sounds
Drawing me close

It's my inner voice,
showing me the path

Seeking And Surrendering

To be in sync
To be in touch

Balanced, worthy,
and always found

The fog has lifted
The road is vivid

There are no hard edges,
when the path is inner

There are no wrong steps,
when true to oneself

I know what the voices are saying
I always knew

The fear is gone
There is only peace

I can hear the whispers of my heart
And they are saying - I need to be me
Whatever may come

Seeking

The Real Me?

Who is the real person behind the smile?
The one behind the laughter, the joy?

Who is the real person behind the sad face?
The one behind the cries, the outbursts?

The many faces of me
The visible and the hidden

The dreams unshared
The stories untold

When can the real me trust?
Where does the real me shine?

How did I let me be lost?
When did I choose to hide?

What is visible is a part of me
What underlies is a part of me

Love binds us all, why the fear?
Isn't it me everywhere?

Seeking And Surrendering

Real and unreal are intertwined
Truth seems hidden but is visible

There is only "I am", and it is us
No need to hide

Unveil what's beneath, here and now
Unveil the real me

Seeking

Questions

Years of searching, asking, yearning
Looking for the glimpse of truth
... for knowing, feeling, clarity
What is the question?
What is the answer?

Questions, no answers, and more questions
Insanity wearing me down, tearing me apart
No restful nights, no healing heart
What is the question?
What is the answer?

The pain is deep, the sadness intense
Emptiness filling every cell
... Nothing else seems to matter
What is the question?
What is the answer?

Churning, turning, yearning with no end in sight
Moving between the real and the dream
Tears running down, joining the ocean
What is the question?
What is the answer?

Seeking And Surrendering

Chills and sweats, chills and sweats
Heart racing, skipping, racing more, stopping
One more question throwing me to the floor
Is this real, is this a dream?
Darkness takes hold, running out of air

...

Then, dark turns into light
Gates open wide, with a lucid path ahead
Answers fill my heart with joy
Churning with no yearning, all knowing
How simple, how real of a dreamlike state

No more questions
Only answers with pure joy

Seeking

Reveal Me

Reveal me,
As I'm forgotten
Deep inward
Hidden
Lost

Reveal me,
As the detachment is painful,
Quietly deafening
Living in the void
Gasping to breathe

Reveal me,
Grasping to claw out
To see the light of truth
As Love awaits
That is pure and whole

Reveal me,
As I'm ready to blossom
To reach to the sky
Spread intoxicating aroma
Filled with the One love

Seeking And Surrendering

Reveal me,
Free me from myself
Release me from the rules and chains
Enlighten me in my remaining days
Let me walk lightly in the air

Reveal me,
As there is so much to give
So much to love
Let me connect
Bind with me thru eternity

Waterfall Or Landing

Caught in the current
Taken to the extremes
Pounding against the rocks
Bleeding and healing, bleeding and healing
Salty taste, feathered with white powdery water
Swimming endlessly
Fearing the day, fearing the night

Where am I heading?
Is it a waterfall?
Is it a landing?

Caught in the whirlpool, going down and down
Breathing in and out
Swimming with the current, swimming against the current
Seeing the trees, grabbing for branches
Swallowing water, Spitting out life
Fearing the day, fearing the night

Where am I heading?
Is it a waterfall?
Is it a landing?

Seeking And Surrendering

Turning over, seeing others turning over
Without livelihood, without passion
One day after next, one night after other
Zombies on the rolling ride
Aimless, game less
Grasping for survival
Fearing the day, fearing the night

Where am I heading?
Is it a waterfall?
Is it a landing?

...

Swallowing the white powdery water
Tasting the salt
Jolting me to life
Floating
Breathing deep
Calming down

Where am I heading?
Is it a waterfall?
Is it a landing?

Thinking of the end
What it might be like
Gazing at the unending sky above

Seeking

With no aspirations
With no attachments
With no expectations
With no judgments

Where am I heading?
Is it a waterfall?
Is it a landing?

Feeling land under my feet
Wondering if a mirage
Cautiously standing up
Seeing far
Unimaginable greatness all around
Sweet beauty in every breath
Serenity in my heart

I am in the clear
On a secure landing
Leaving the waterfall far behind

No more swirling aimlessly
No more fear
Enjoying the gift
With open heart, with clear mind
Just being
It is heaven all around

Seeking And Surrendering

Seeking Connection

Wrote some poetry from the heart
Words poured out through my soul onto the pen
Don't Know the source or why they disappeared
Felt the inspiration and now it's gone

Wishing everlasting magic, as I feel lost in the illusion
Sensed a connection, the touch
Now the ego has returned, wearing me down
Need that mystical music to connect and reconnect

Need that deep dark of the night, the quiet, the stillness
My lost soul needs the poems to open up my heart
Entrusting my spirit into the naked air
Laying all out, no truth held back

Hearing me and healing me through and through
Let me stay connected now and forever
It's an unending desire for that hidden truth
Without that magic, I am neither here nor there

Back in the illusion, I hear the music once more
Starting to awaken, and words gush out
Letting me in the know through all moments
Feeling the calm, feeling inspired, and connected once more

Let Go

Let go today
Of all the desires
Of all the sadness
Of all the dark shadows lurking in your dreams

Let go now
Of the regrets
Of the mistakes
Of the disappointments

Let go and forget
The angry words
The awful thoughts
The missteps

Let go and breathe
Free from all the wins
Free from all the haves
Free of all the triumphs

Let go and love
With no masks
With no pretenses
With all giving from the heart

Seeking And Surrendering

Let go and live
For each moment
For the wonder
For the awe

Let go forever
All accepting
All creating
All joy

Do You Want To Be?

Do you want to be happy?
I can show you how

Do you want to be sad?
I can give you reasons

Do you want to be angry?
I can compel you

Do you want to feel loved?
Let me count the ways

Do you want to be connected?
Let's whirl and meditate

...

You can be what you wish
But you have to believe

Just choose quickly,
Cause life goes by in a blink

Seeking And Surrendering

You Are

You are
You have been
Forever will be

Who you were born to be
Who you think you are
Who you wish to be

...

Think as you want to be
Speak as you want to be
Dream as you want to be

Believe who you want to be
Live who you want to be
Be the gift you are meant to be

Fleeting Moments

I live for the fleeting moments

When I have clarity
When I feel pure love
When the clouds disappear
When my heart opens up
When the mind sees purity
When the verses flow from me

I live for these moments
Oh, but so fleeting ...

Ponder

Do you ponder or live life?
What's worth your time?
Living life to the fullest or
wondering what life is about?

Happy to be here
Happy to enjoy each day
To enjoy each moment, as I stroll

This wind that blows through the trees
The squeaking branches and the crackling leaves
The horses in the meadow eating hay

The warmth of the sun on my skin
The clouds in the sky, passing by
The airplane far above leaving a trail

Sitting in loneliness is deafening
Wandering around, feeling the world
Enlightenment is in the experience

Seeking

Being in the world

To observe

To see

To hear

To learn

To laugh

To play

To wonder

To be amazed

Life is a blessing, whether real or not

Live it while the story unfolds

Seeking And Surrendering

Empty Your Cup

Empty your cup,
So that your heart feels pain of wondrous love

Empty your cup,
So that your mind is clear from gray clouds

Empty your cup,
So that your life is filled with joy

Empty your cup,
So that your days turn into meaningful light

Empty your cup,
So that your nights turn into star filled skies

Empty your cup,
So that your smile brightens all hearts

Empty your cup,
So that your sleepless nights turn in into playful melodies

Empty your cup,
So that you can fill each day with new life

Seeking

Empty your cup,

So that your soul awakens to the truth

Empty your cup,

So that your cup may forever be refilled ·····

Seeking And Surrendering

Come In

Come in with an open mind
With arms ready to embrace
With a warm heart

Come in with imagination ready to fly
With joy that can spread like wildfire
With sorrow ready for healing

It's time to observe the invisible shadows
It's time to go within
It's time to let go

It's a place to love all
It's a place to be one
Come in to unfold

Appreciation And Connection

Seeking And Surrendering

Who You Are ...

Who you are is a piece of God
Playing on this vast land

Strumming guitar strings
Dancing to a tune you write

Having a blessed life
Relearning who you are

Until you wake up again
To the life beyond

Appreciation And Connection

Living in Amazement

I live in amazement of
The beauty of each day
The morning dew
The brightness of the sun
The air that envelopes me
The body that breathes
The eyes that see
The heart that feels

I live in amazement of
Those who lead with kindness
Those who build with strength
Those who give boundlessly
Those who paint beauty
Those who sing with joy
Those who give blessings from the soul
Those who live to love

Seeking And Surrendering

I live in amazement of
The doctor who heals wounds
The lawman who saves lives
The author who writes prose
The fighter who calms the fire
The custodian who cleans our space
The pilot who shortens distances
The scientist who discovers the unknown

I live in amazement of
The emptiness I feel
The anger I show
The forgiving hearts
All that I've learned
The difference that I made
The days gone by
The forgotten memories

I live in amazement of
What I see
What I feel
What I hear
What I give
What I take
Those I love
The life I live

Appreciation And Connection

I live in amazement

In awe

In tears

In joy

In jolts

In hope

In shadows

In light

I live in amazement of the story of this life ⋯⋯

Seeking And Surrendering

Eternity

In the eternity we're from
There's only love
Multidimensional awareness
Oneness

In the eternity we're from
There's connectedness
Peaceful solitude
Boundless clarity

In the eternity we're from
There's no time
No worries
No limits

In the eternity we're from
Joy is abound
Contentment
Fulfillment

In the eternity we're from
We're all brothers and sisters
All energy
All light

Appreciation And Connection

In the eternity we're from
Our lives are memories
Created at whim
Blown in the vacuum of space

In the eternity we're from
There's no regret
There's no fear
There's only the beauty of One Love

Floating

Freely floating

Floating freely

Flying

Skipping

Whistling

Kissing

The beauty

The colors

The sparkles

The waves

Splashing

Playing

Joining

Loving

Floating happily

Happily floating

Appreciation And Connection

Moments Are Passing

Moments are passing, feeling alone
All those around, connected somehow

Say you love them, take the time
Pick up the phone, make the call

Wish happy birthdays, wish happy days
Check on loved ones, on those in need

Say your hellos, say your goodbyes
Learn every day, give back what you can

Gifts are abound, spread them around
So many wishes, share your heart

Say your thanks, hear the echo
Feel the love around, spread it wide

The storyline is time bound, love is timeless
Moments are passing, you're everlasting

Be the love!

Seeking And Surrendering

I Bow

I bow to the majestic mountains
To the mighty oceans
To the vast sky

I bow to my loving heart
To my mysterious soul
To this miraculous body

I bow to the beginning
To the end
To the illusion in between

I bow with tears of joy
I bow with bewilderment
I bow in awe

I bow humbly, still in search of the One Love

Appreciation And Connection

Except Yours?

At nights, in loneliness, in quietness
What can I yearn for, except your closeness?

In weakness, in lapses, in missteps
What can I pray for, except your forgiveness?

In worries, in fears, in sadness
What can calm me, except your glorious presence?

With uncertainties, the bitterness, and losses
What can heal me, except a world of your mercy?

In the jungles, in the meadows, by the streams
What can I be grateful for, except your creations?

In the twilight, in the sunrise, and the sunset
What can I do, except to live the blessed-filled days?

In yesterday, today, and tomorrow,
What can I devote to, except longing for knowing you?

Seeking And Surrendering

Have faith

Have faith in yourself, that you are from God
That God is with you at all times

Have faith in your breath, that it is worthy to breathe
That you are health, healing, and whole

Have faith in your presence, that you are empowered
That your words can bring peace

Have faith in yourself, that your struggles are holy
That the mountains of fear have rivers flowing with joy

Have faith in your eyes, that there are many shades to the
*   blue sky*
That the moon illuminates the dark nights

Have faith in your heart, that people are kind
That your love creates love

Have faith in your life, that your amazing destiny awaits
That your belief casts the net that defines life

Appreciation And Connection

Have faith in yourself, that you can make your story bright
That this is the tale to be told for eternity

Have faith in your might, that you can live to the fullest
That on this day you know you are the truth

Have faith

Seeking And Surrendering

Wondering By The Lake

Wondering by the lake
Absorbing what surrounds me

Hearing my heartbeat
The chirping of the sparrows

Watching the white birds swoop into the lake
The mighty eagle soaring above

Feeling the cool breeze brushing against my hair
The sun spreading its bright setting colors

The beauty is breathtaking
The moment is precious

Connecting with all that surrounds
Connecting with all that is beyond

With an unending gaze into the sky
I wish this moment would never end

Thankful and humble
Wondering by the lake

Part Of A Whole

Seeking And Surrendering

What's Beyond

What's beyond that beautiful smile?
That beautiful cloud formation?
That mother hugging her child?
That roaring lightning in the sky?
That drunken tumble?
That raging river?
That colorful rainbow?
That laughter from the heart?
That birth of a newborn?
That deeply sad cry of loss?

All amaze me
Humble me
Tear deep into my heart
Shock me
Numb me
Take my breath away
Knock me unconscious
Float me for eternity
Guide me till I reach the beyond

Part Of A Whole

Knowing Purpose

Does the tree branch know it is part of the tree?
Does the sunset know that it is painting the sky?

Does the rose flower know of its intoxicating aroma?
Does the tree leaf know it turns red and falls?

Does the ocean know it encompasses the vast marine life?
Does the desert know its sandstorms parade the dry land?

Does the cobblestone know it is worn down by millions of
  footsteps?
Does the rail track know its destination to magical lands?

Do you know your purpose in the world?
Do you know how you're embraced by all that surrounds?

Do you know that you are loved?
Do you know that you are love?

Seeking And Surrendering

I Am From

I am from the ocean
From the sand
From the air surrounding us

I am from the Sun
From the moon
From the galaxies near and far

I am from the unending joy
From the unending beauty
From the unending love that's within us

I am from the abundance
From the ever after
From forever and ever that is us

Part Of A Whole

Reality Or Dream

Reality circles into the dream
Dream circles into reality

Which is real, which is not?
Is it a twist or a knot?

Can I dream of reality?
Can I live in a dream?

Dreaming of a clear day
Reality is filled with dreams

Am I awake or dreaming?
Am I waking up to the dream?

Is life in the dream?
Is the dream my life?

Shake me from dreaming
Shake me out of reality

The real dream is beautiful
Woven all around us

Seeking And Surrendering

It's all real

It's all a dream

It's all for us

Dream inspired

Part Of A Whole

Illusion

Is this an illusion?
Particles shaped like me, like you
A fantasy beyond belief
An unending story, that evolves, repeats

Is this an illusion?
Forging an alliance of thoughts
Creating, loving, expanding, collapsing
No boundaries, no walls

Is this an illusion?
For me and you, or for me alone
Looking around, touching nothing, touching everything
Feeling, hearing, sensing, smelling, swallowing, loving

Is this an illusion?
Am I walking on fallen leaves?
Am I breathing air or there is no air to breathe?
Am I here, there, nowhere, everywhere?

Is this an illusion?
Nothing is real, nothing is there to touch
It feels so lonely, a prison all around
Can I break free? To what I don't know

Seeking And Surrendering

Is this an illusion?
Never ending, surrounding me
Swallowing me, challenging me, loving me
I see the shadows behind the sky, watching me, calling on me

Open-up and break free
Take the plunge and fly around
Create it, live it, love it, breathe it, consume it, spread it
The illusion is magic, the illusion is real, the illusion is me

Part Of A Whole

The Inevitable

Trying to understand
That which I don't see
But is there
That which I don't hear
But speaks to me

Waiting patiently,
For my time to surrender without resistance
To see and sense all
To allow without fear
To embrace with love

To wholly know,
All that ever was
All that is
All that forever will be
The inevitable answer hidden inside

Man-Made, God-Made

Overwhelms me to think,
What I am looking at
Is there a distinction?

Man-made, God-made
I wish I could understand
Who the creator is

What is the inspiration?
A dream, a vision?
Whose idea was it?

Does it matter?
Do I have to know?
Couldn't I just enjoy?

It is brilliance
It is beauty
It is a miracle

Tangible or intangible
A tree or a structure
A spice or medicine

Part Of A Whole

A river or a canal
A dream or a movie
Life as we know it

Intertwined, timeless
Parallels, boundless
Amazing, amazing

Seeking And Surrendering

Faces

Billion faces of God surround this earth
Do you see the one God?

Breathing, staring, talking
Do you feel the connectedness?

Being born, living, dying
Do you sense the point in each?

Suffering, selfishness, hurt
Why do you keep losing face?

Happiness, kindness, laughter
Are you in harmony with your soul?

The oneness is the truth
The ego is the illusion that undermines the truth

Choosing to heal or choosing to hurt
Still doesn't change what is

Turn your back on the illusion,
See the face in the mirror

Look deep into the faces and know that you are not alone
That we are all connected, in one face

Part Of A Whole

Nowhere Land

Where there is no end, no beginning
Where there is only love, boundless joy

Where no one knows their origin, but feels alive
Where you see the shadows, but can't reach thru the veil

Where you belong, but can't touch thru this realm
Where your dreams are about, but your mind plays games

Where you yearn to be all your life, but don't know why
Where your heart pounds for, and can't be calmed

Where you are one, and all is you
Where heaven is life, and life is heaven

Where you are truth and beauty
Where you are love, and loved

Where you are welcomed and blessed
Where you are all, and feel whole

This nowhere land is near
This nowhere land is within

Seeking And Surrendering

Behind The Eyes

Who is behind the eyes in the mirror
The soul behind the face
The meaning behind the words?

Who is behind the sound in the voice
The beat hidden in the heart
The love behind the hurt?

Who is behind the joy in the laughter
The sadness behind the tears
The tension behind the burst?

Who is behind the curve in the twist
The lines on the worn hands
The wrinkles on the face of time?

Who is behind the waves over the ocean bed
The wind howling in the night
The clouds in the blue sky?

Who is behind the seeds beneath the sprouts
The barks on the tree trunk
The emptiness in space?

Part Of A Whole

Who is behind the blossom hidden in the bud
The Caterpillar before the butterfly
The fetus forming into an old man?

Who is behind the me in me
The you in you
The them in them?

Who is behind the body
Behind the action
Behind the results?

Who is behind the space
Behind the land
Behind the hope?

Who is me?
Who is us?
Who is One?

Seeking And Surrendering

Complicated

It all seems so complicated
Is it all my imagination?
Is it all an illusion?

It's a magical show
On a beautiful clever set
With clueless actors

So much to live for
So much to die for
So many causes

So much to learn
So much to do
So much to taste

What's the truth?
What's reality?
Am I dreaming a lifetime?

I want to stop running in the maze
I want to stop playing the games
It all seems so complicated

Part Of A Whole

Maybe the truth sits in the shadows
In the turns and twists of the maze
Visible only with an open mind

Am I ready for the truth yet?
Can I handle the implications?
Can I give up all that I think I know?

Maybe I should play the game a little longer
Keep running in this beautiful complicated maze
Maybe the answers will be visible tomorrow ...

Seeking And Surrendering

Does It Feel?

Do the dead miss their grieving family?
Do the fish freely swim to be there for the fishermen?
Do the cows care for the farmer's long days under the sun?

Do the plants feel the kindness of their Gardner?
Do the trees warmly embrace the crowded jungle?
Does the grass appreciate the sun shining bright?

Does the brush yearn for the stroke that creates art?
Does the wood need to be carved into a masterpiece?
Does the clay anxiously await to be formed?

Does the rock cry for the erosion over time?
Does the leaf feel gratitude towards its roots?
Does the ocean gasp at the force of its tsunami?

Does the cloud sense the time to form for the rain?
Does the rain woefully flood the narrow streams?
Does the dessert long for the downpouring rain?

Part Of A Whole

Does the ego fear how special we all are?
Does the mind tremble by how endless infinity is?
Does the heart sense how boundless love is?

Does God weep for seeming unreachable?
Does my soul feel how close I am with the One?
Do I live so that I can lament for the unknown?

Seeking And Surrendering

Don't Get Caught In The Story

The story is just a story
Don't get caught in the mini lines
Don't let the tough moments take your joy
Don't let your heart fill with sorrow
Don't let this moment drag you down

Why this?
Why here?
Why today?
Why them?
Why me?

Who's narrating the woven stories?
Who's the drifter on the street?
Who's the lady sitting on the park bench?
Who's the joyful child playing on the grass?
Who's filling your heart with love?

All connected
All in harmony
All yours to create
All yours to experience
All yours to perceive

Part Of A Whole

This was today's story
Tomorrow will have another to tell
Don't get caught in the story line
It's just part of a grand production
The beauty is in all the stories combined

Create
Observe
Laugh
Throw away
Surrender

Maybes

Maybe it's good news
Maybe its bad news

Maybe it's meant to be
Or maybe you made it that way

Maybe you're to be a leader
Or maybe a follower

Maybe he's the right person for you
Maybe you're the wrong person for him

Maybe you're meant to fly
Maybe the ground is where you thrive

Maybe the sky is the limit
Maybe we're from a limitless world

Maybe you're always sad
Maybe a smile is your choice

Maybe your world turned upside down
Maybe it's your point of view

Part Of A Whole

Maybe time goes by too fast
Maybe time is an illusion

Maybe it is all overwhelming
Maybe it's time for intermission ...

I Am A Piece Of A Whole

I am from the sun,
One ray shining on

I am from the moon,
That brightness, a piece of that face

I am from the ocean,
One drop from the waves

I am from the land, the beach,
One grain of sand

I am from the vast sky,
One bubble of a white cloud

I am from the jungle,
A branch on a tree

I am from the space between us,
One breath, in and out

I am here, now
I am everyone, one with all

Part Of A Whole

Stories

I live a story
With dreams and realities hard to discern
A life tightly woven but unraveling day by day

I read stories told by those who share
Of lives well lived, of hardships, of ills and wins
Interwoven lives that affect all

I watch movies
Created by story tellers about imagined characters
Drawing vivid unlived lives

I create art
A vision in color, on a blank canvas
A concept, a message, an impression in time

I tell stories of how I see life
Stories that are felt, and
Some believed, crafted from a point of view

I keep seeking the story that is the Truth
Un-imposed, un-interpreted, un-embellished
The unmasked eternal story of us ...